WATER TRANSPORT

Alistair Hamilton-MacLaren

Illustrations by John Yates

Wayland

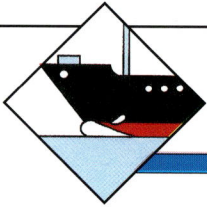

Exploring Technology

Communications
Flight
Houses and Homes
Land Transport
Machines
Structures
Textiles
Water Transport

Series editor: William Wharfe
Book editor: Hazel Songhurst
Designer: Malcolm Walker, Kudos Designs

Cover: *A powerboat speeds across the water with such force that it throws up spray as it travels.*

First published in 1991 by
Wayland (Publishers) Ltd
61 Western Road, Hove
East Sussex BN3 1JD, England

**British Library Cataloguing in
Publication Data**
Hamilton-MacLaren, Alistair
  Water transport. – (Exploring
  technology)
  I. Title   II. Series
  623.8

ISBN 0–7502–0161–4

Phototypeset by Kalligraphic Design Ltd,
Horley, Surrey
Printed in Italy by G. Canale & C.S.p.A.
Bound in France by A.G.M.

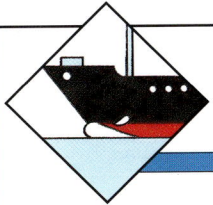

Contents

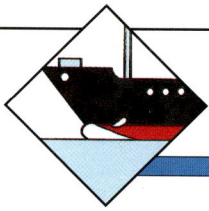

Water and people

To enjoy water activities safely, it is a good idea to join a club.

Water has always been essential to life. Since nearly two-thirds of the world's surface is covered with water, we are always in close contact with it. Where water is scarce, such as in desert regions, very few living things are able to survive.

Most civilizations settled beside water and so it was natural for it to be used in many ways. Water supplied the power to turn shafts that worked machinery. It was essential for growing plants for food, and a perfect means of transporting large and heavy loads.

Today, water pollution is a huge concern. We can all do our bit to help by using environmentally friendly detergents and other products in the home. We should also dispose of any form of chemical and oil products thoughtfully.

Water can be very dangerous! Never play alone near water. Be especially careful near currents, either inland or by the sea. Learn to swim and take part in life-saving and survival classes if you can. If you go out in a boat, always wear an approved life-preserver.

If you see an accident, stay calm but act swiftly. Tell an adult, or find a phone and ring the emergency number. The coastguard, ranger or the police must be told exactly what happened and where.

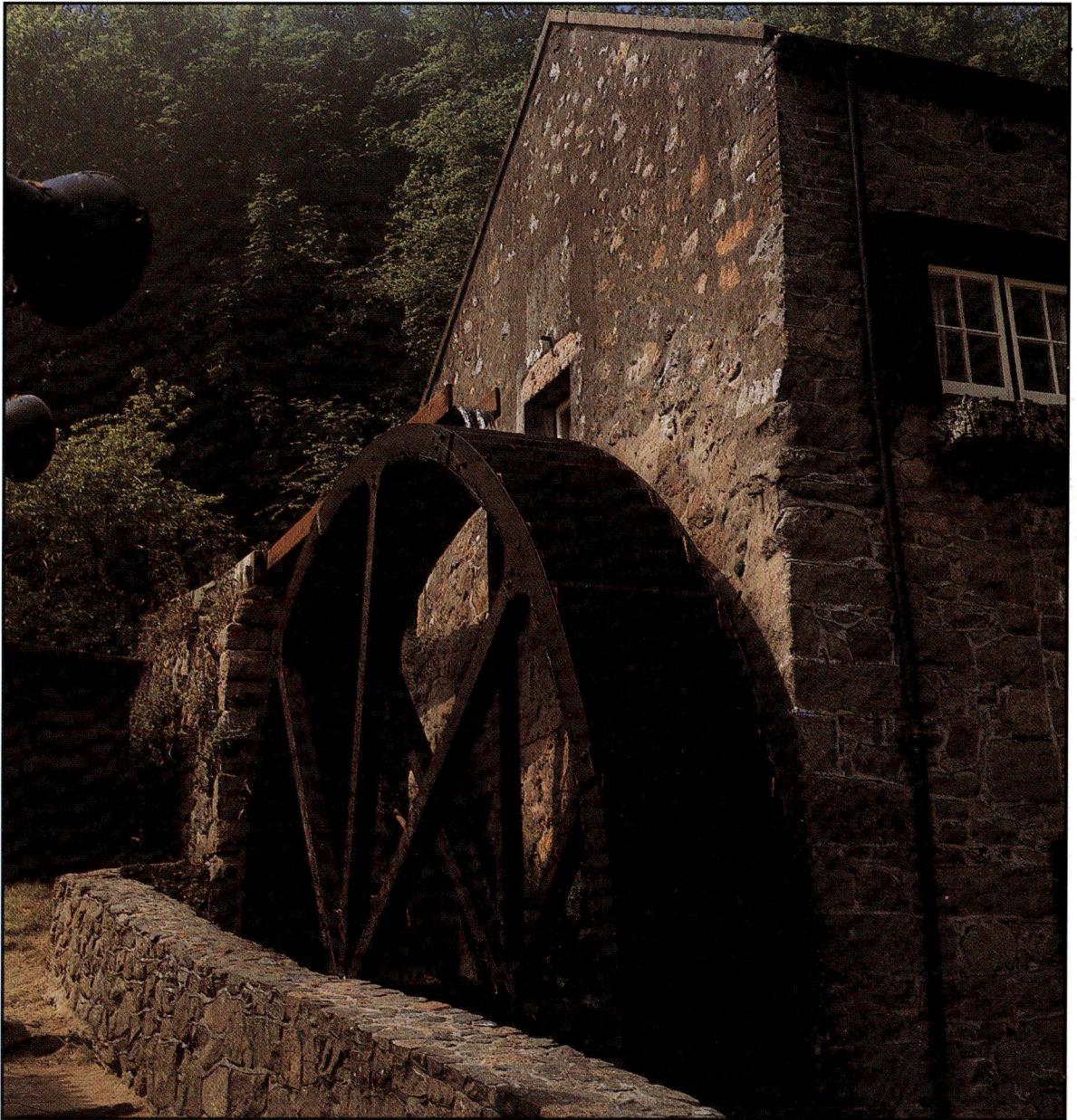

Watermills have been used for centuries to power machinery.

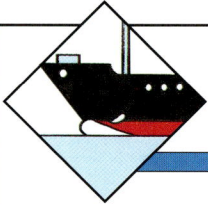

Floating

There are two ways that objects can float:

1. Any object will float as long as it is lighter than the liquid that it is placed in. Timber will float in water until it becomes saturated and too heavy.

2. By shaping a material that is heavier than a liquid in a particular way, it is possible to make it float. Glass fishing-floats and metal and concrete boats are classic examples of this.

The following scientific principle was first stated by the Greek mathematician, Archimedes:

'Provided that a vessel (boat) displaces (takes up the volume space of) its own weight of liquid then the vessel will float.'

To make boats, we use materials that are heavier than water, such as steel or concrete. It is the way in which the material is shaped that stops it from sinking. Next time you visit a harbour or marina, look carefully at the shapes of the boats moored there. The space inside a boat's hull is mostly air. Air is much lighter than water and provided a boat is not overloaded, this also helps it to float safely.

Floating buoys are used to mark navigation channels and warn of sunken wrecks.

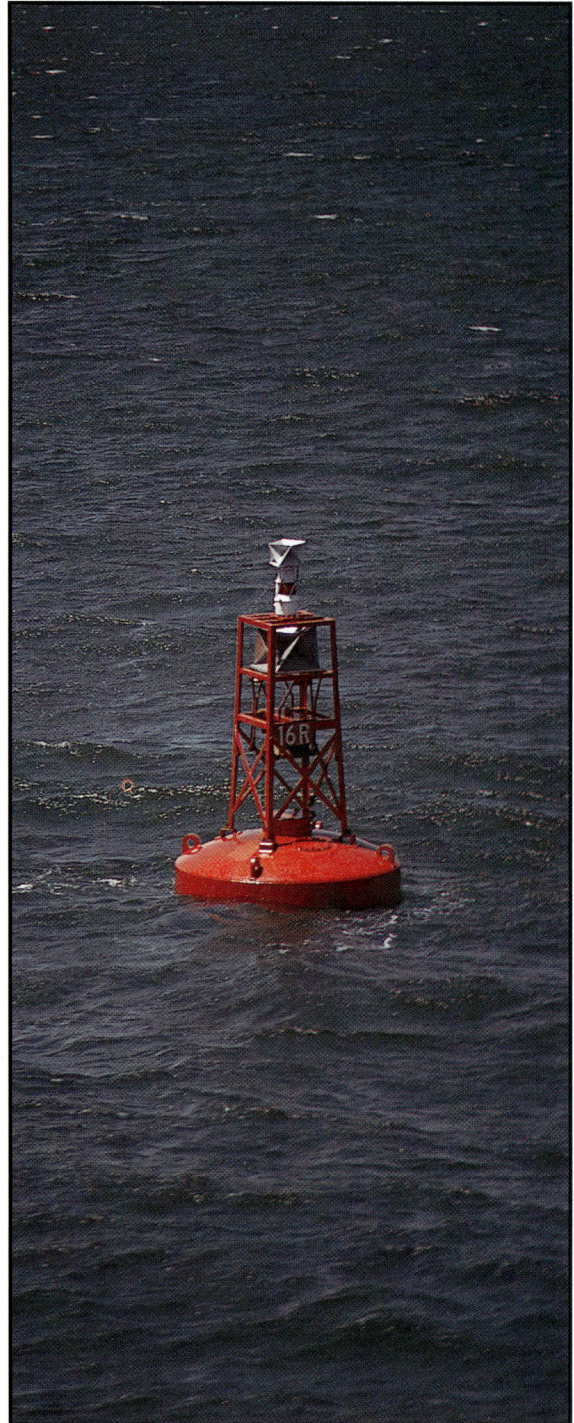

Floating experiment

Scientific experiments are used to collect information, or data. Large quantities of this data are needed before conclusions can be drawn. It is important that data is always accurate.

You need:

Large bucket of water
Types of wood (twigs, balsa strips, pine cubes, wood blocks)
Other materials and shapes: cork, paper,
metal, rubber, china (cup or saucer), plastic, glass
Eureka can and small glass jar
Balance beam
Net of marbles
Paper, pencil, ruler

1. Make a chart like the first one shown. See which materials and objects float and which sink in the bucket of water. Fill in the results on the chart. Which sinking materials float if they are a certain shape?

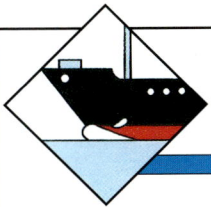

1. Sheet.1.

MATERIAL	FLOATS	SINKS	NOTES
Wood			
twig			
block			
pine cube			
balsa strip			
other materials			
cork			
glass			
feather			

2. Choose a good floater. Place it in the Eureka can full to the brim with water. Sink it slowly and catch the water overflow in the small jar.

2. floater / Eureka can

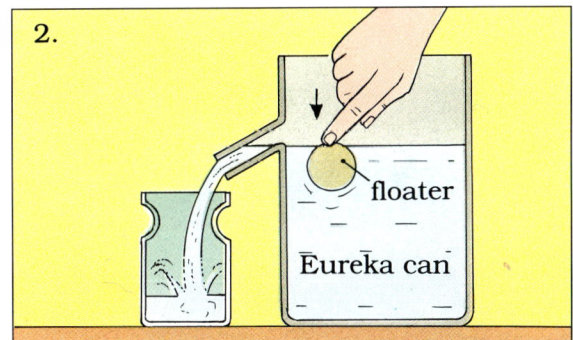

3. Attach the bag of marbles to the floater. Use a balance beam to balance the weight of the water in the jar with the floater and marbles.

4. safe cargo load / balance a corked test-tube to float at any level

4. Test your result in the bucket of water as shown. Choose different floaters and record your results on a second chart.

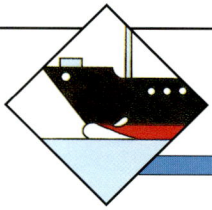

The first boats

The earliest-known evidence of boats comes from stone carvings made approximately 6,000 years ago by ancient peoples.

The earliest water craft were probably floating logs that people sat astride or clung to, but these must have been very unstable and difficult to control. The next development was to hollow out tree trunks to make simple canoes. This was an enormous task for early people, who only had very crude hand tools. Timber was hacked from the middle of the tree trunk with flint axes and burned away, using carefully controlled fires. These hollowed-out canoes made fairly stable craft that travelled fast through the water. They could carry people and cargo from one place to another.

North American Indians developed a method of stripping the complete bark of a birch tree in one piece. They would mount it onto a light framework of wooden spars, held together with lacings made from animal skins. These canoes, although fragile, were capable of carrying huge loads along fast-flowing rivers. When waterfalls interrupted the route, the light

Pacific islanders carving a canoe where the tree was felled.

A modern, two-person glass-fibre kayak keeps these people afloat.

canoes could be unloaded and carried around to the next suitable stretch of river.

Much further north, the Inuit developed a different type of canoe. These were single-seater kayaks, made from seal skins stretched over frameworks of timber and bone. Kayaks are still in use today. The person riding the kayak is tightly laced in. Skilled canoeists are able to turn their kayaks right over in the water and back up again, and hardly get wet! The kayaks are used for hunting seal and special two-bladed paddles enable hunters to travel quickly far out to sea.

For hundreds of years, Welsh fishermen used coracles – tiny boats made of tarred canvas stretched over a framework of hazelwood. They fished on rapid rivers with long nets. At the end of the day the coracle was lifted on to the owner's back and carried home.

Today, modern materials such as aluminium and glass-fibre are used to build canoes, but the basic design has changed very little.

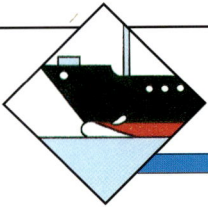

Make a paper boat

You need:
Stiff cartridge paper
  (200 mm x 200 mm)

1. Fold the paper in half from corner to corner. Fold in half again, then unfold the whole sheet.

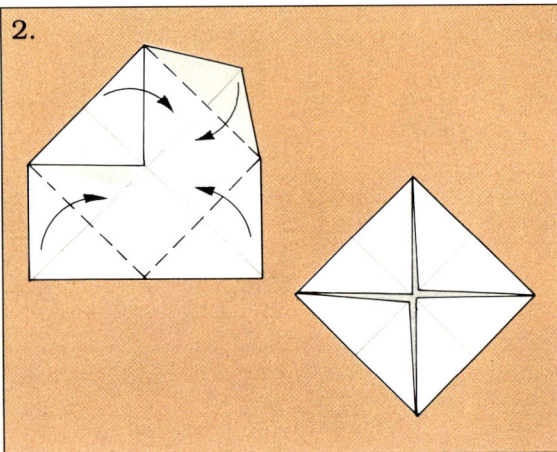

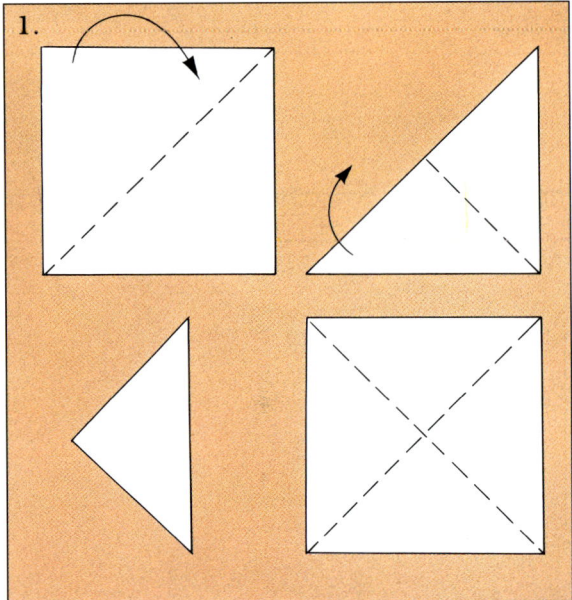

1.

2. Using the fold lines to guide you, fold the corners into the middle.

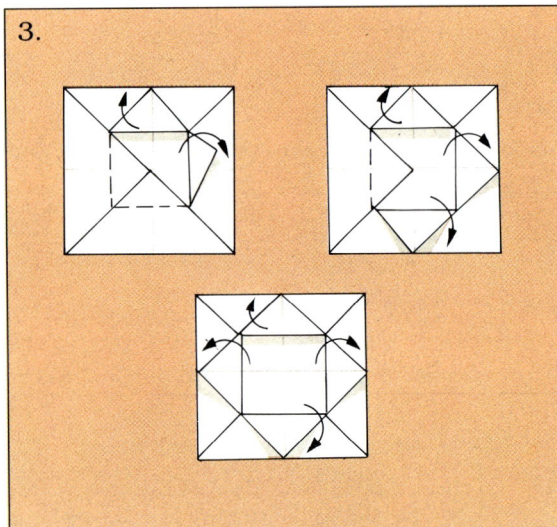

3. Fold the corners from the middle back to the edges.

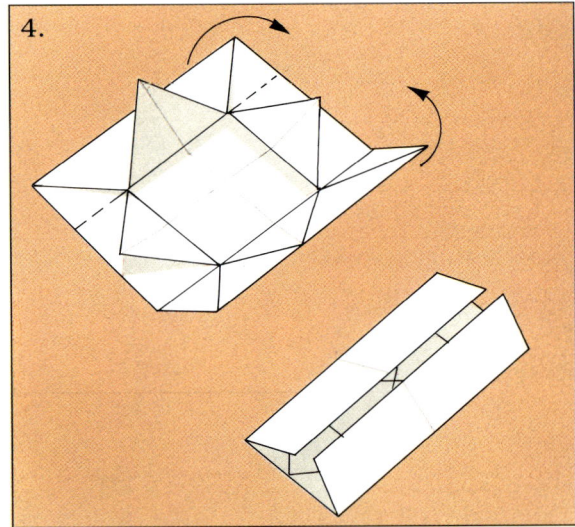

4. Fold over two sides into the middle, to make an oblong shape.

10

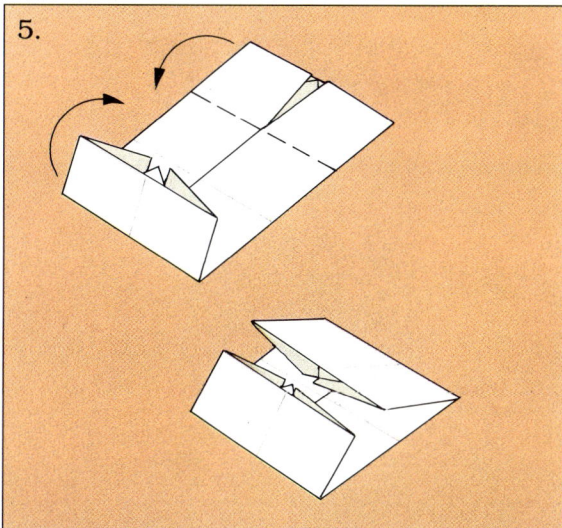

5. Fold over the short sides into the middle.

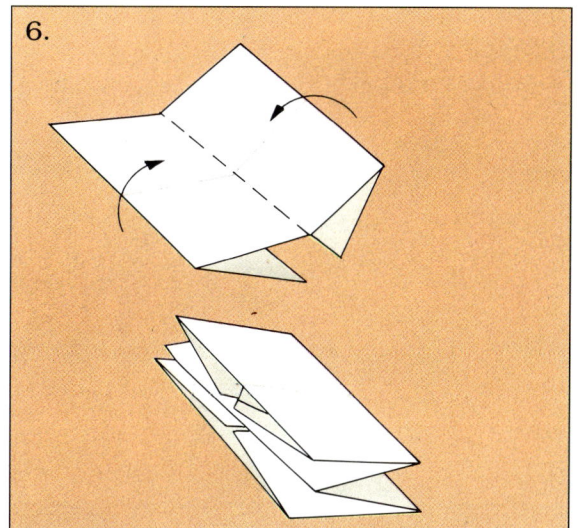

6. Turn over the paper and fold it in half.

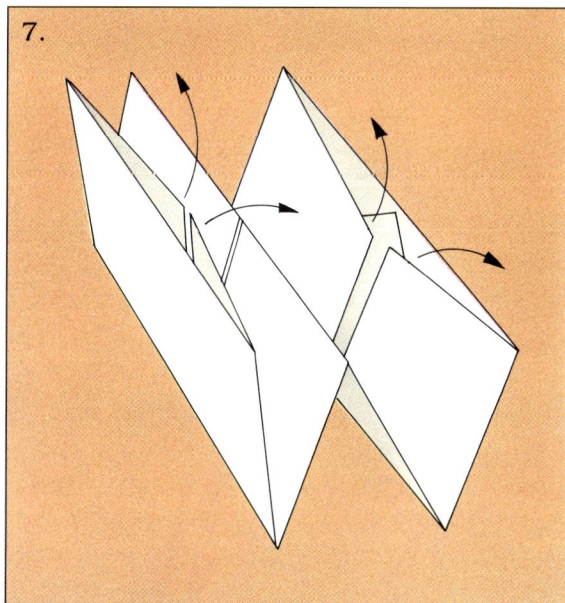

7. Open it up slightly and gently pull out the four corner flaps to make the boat.

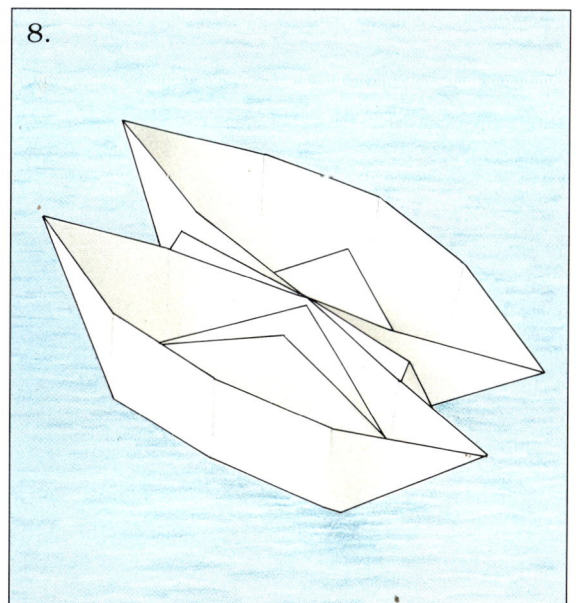

8. Test your boat on water.

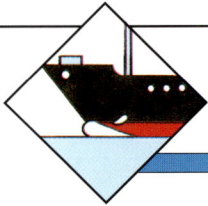

Rafts

In 1947, the Norwegian, Thor Heyerdahl, crossed the Pacific Ocean on the raft *Kon Tiki*. Made of balsa wood, the *Kon Tiki* was based on craft built and used by Polynesians. In 1970, Heyerdahl crossed the Atlantic Ocean on a raft made of papyrus reed, proving without doubt, that ancient civilizations had the ability to cross oceans and colonize new regions of the world.

Rafts remained in use for hundreds of years, often to ferry people across rivers. Where a raft was used to cross a river with a strong current, it was common to stretch a rope tightly from one bank to the other. The raft would be connected to the rope with loops. The raft could then be poled or hauled by rope across the river without being

In remote areas rafts are still used as ferries.

swept downstream by the current.

Today, rafts are used mainly as emergency rescue equipment on boats and aircraft. On ships, they are often stored on deck in round white drums. In an emergency, when the drum hits the water, a cylinder of compressed gas automatically inflates the raft. Survival rafts are bright yellow or bright orange so that they can be spotted easily from the air. Equipped with emergency supplies, a first-aid kit, distress flares and often a radio transmitter, they can support their occupants for many days. What do you think should be included in the survival kit of a four-person life raft?

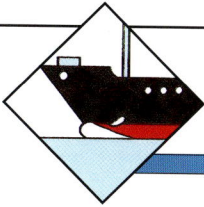

Make a detergent boat

You need:
Balsa wood strip
   (100 mm x
   45 mm)
Modelling knife
Glass-paper
Pencil and ruler
Thick detergent

1. Draw the outline of the boat on the balsa wood following the measurements shown.

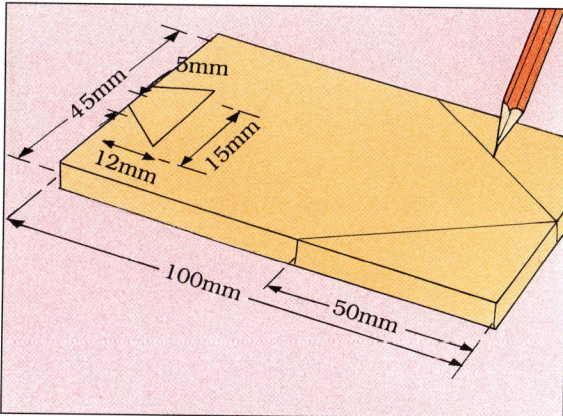

2. Work on a cutting board to cut out the boat. Cut against the grain of the wood. Remember to cut away from you to prevent accidents. Smooth the boat to a streamlined shape with glass-paper.

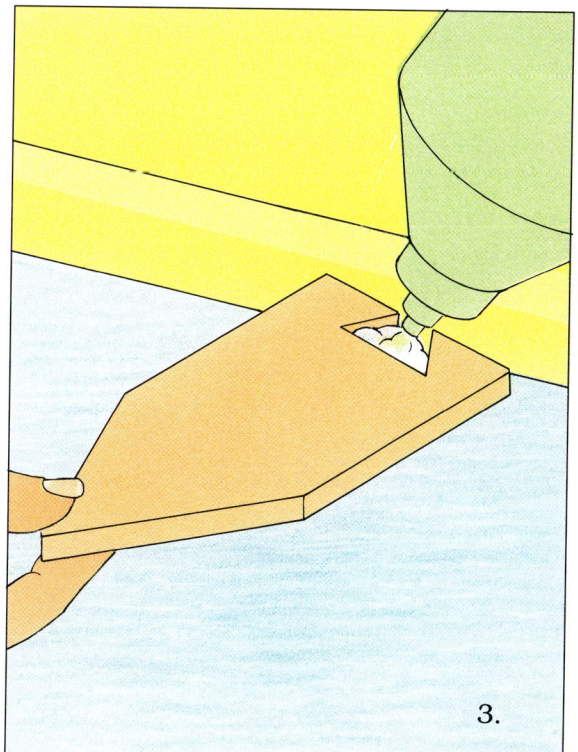

3. Place the boat on clean, still water in a large bowl or bath. Squeeze a drop of detergent in the trap at the back of the boat. The boat will shoot forwards.

When the water is covered with a layer of detergent, the boat will no longer move. You need clean water, free from soap, to make it work again.

More ideas
Design and make a rudder underneath the boat to control the direction in which it travels.

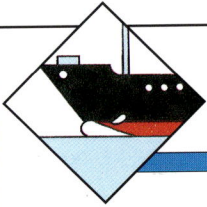

Paddles and oars

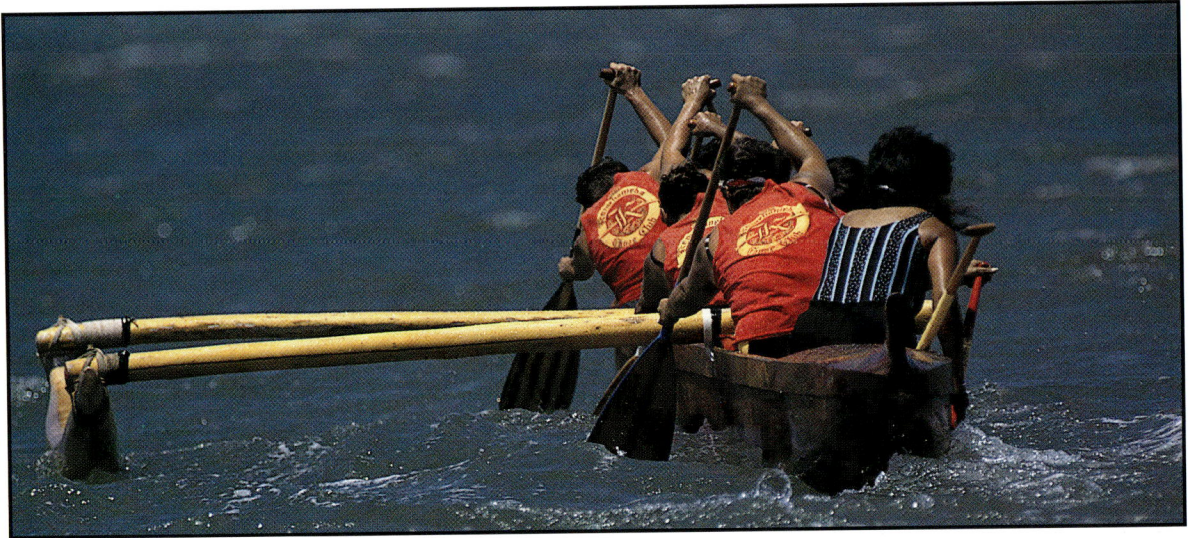

Drifting craft only travel in the direction of the water current or the wind. The need to make boats travel in other directions led to the development of paddles, poles and oars.

Poles are used in fairly shallow, still waters to propel boats along. The operator sometimes walks the length of the boat pushing the pole against the river or canal bed.

Paddles are levers that pull against the water, moving the boat forwards. The fulcrum (pivot point) of the paddle is the lower hand of the person paddling. In a kayak, where it is difficult to change hand positions when changing paddling sides, a combined two-bladed paddle is used.

Oars, or sweeps, are also levers that pull against the water to move a boat forwards, but here the

The canoe outrigger gives stability to the boat in the surf. The boat is steered at the stern using a paddle.

fulcrum is a pivot point on the side of the boat, known as rowlocks or crutches.

About 4,000 years ago the ancient Egyptians built large galley ships powered by banks of oars. The oars were worked by slaves chained to the decks, several to each oar.

Although many attempts have been made to design systems that allow rowers to face the direction that they are travelling, this has not been successful and the basic system remains the same. Rowing is a highly effective method of moving on water. Modern lightweight skiffs with sliding seats glide fast through the water.

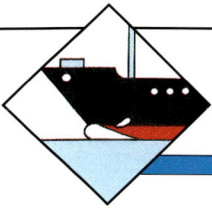

Make a war-canoe

You need:

Small, straight tree
  branches
Modelling knife
Glass-paper

Clear varnish
Strong twine
Modelling clay or
  Plasticine

1. Make the canoe from the thickest branch. Use a modelling knife to take off the bark and whittle it into shape. Hollow out the canoe (small cuts work best). Always cut away from yourself. Keep both hands behind the blade. Use glass-paper to smooth the final shape.

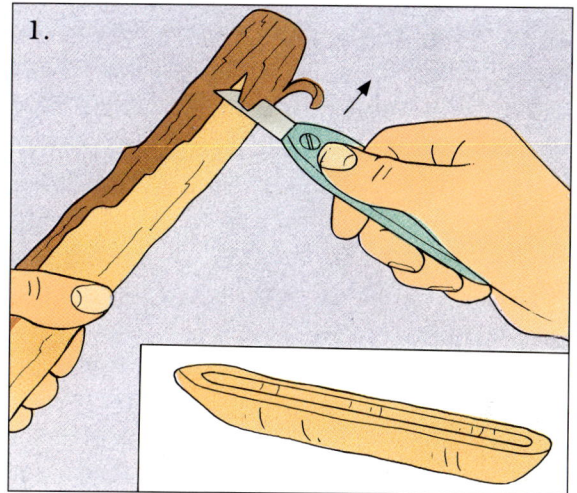

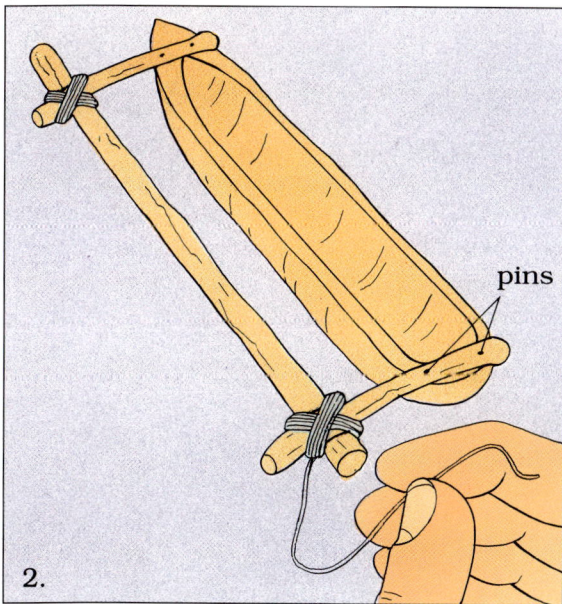

1.

2. Cut and shape the outrigger with the modelling knife and glass-paper. Tie the outrigger to the canoe with twine. Seal the twine in place with clear varnish.

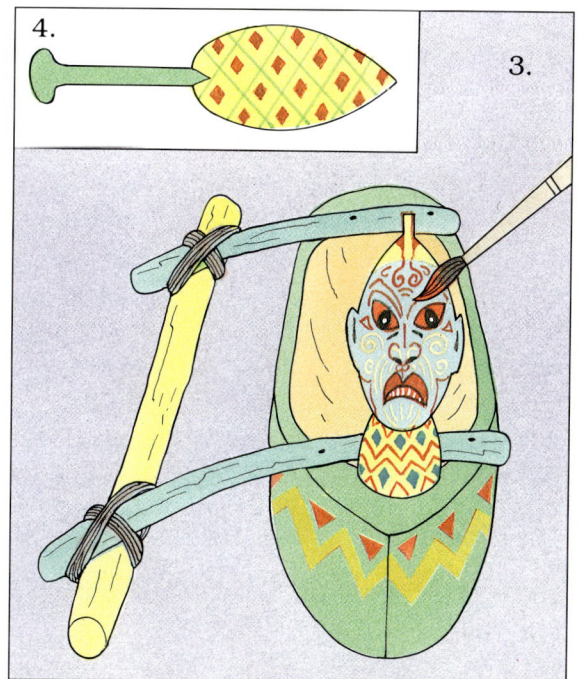

pins

2.

3. Make a fearsome figurehead warrior from the clay or Plasticine. Mount it on the front of the canoe.
4. Cut and shape a wooden paddle if you like. Decorate the paddle and the canoe with brightly painted designs.

4.

3.

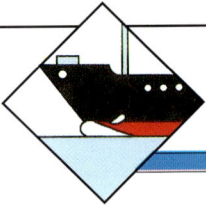

Sail power

The first sails hung from masts were little more than squares of canvas that helped boats move faster when a favourable wind was blowing from behind. When a mast is added to a boat, the stability of the boat in the water is changed. To compensate for the pressure of the wind on the mast – which could turn the boat over – two common methods were used to make boats more stable. Either the boat was built with a deep, weighted keel or the boat or ship was made with more than one hull, to widen the load area. Keel boats required deep anchorages, but multi-hull boats were less manoeuvrable and could normally only manage small cargoes. The ability to resist being capsized meant that boats could now sail across the wind, and by a process known as 'tacking', they could zig-zag back and forth to

Early adventurers sailed in boats with crude navigational systems.

Tiny feluccas with large sails travel swiftly along the River Nile.

their chosen destination. On small boats or on inland waters, tacking resulted in a change of direction every few minutes. Out at sea, on a large ship, each tack could last for several hours.

As technology developed, ships became larger, faster and capable of carrying huge cargoes. During the sixteenth and seventeenth centuries foreign colonies were established and overseas trade developed. Much of the trade was very valuable: gold, silver, oriental silks and spices. To protect trading ships and colonies, warships too became faster and better equipped.

Sending large quantities of goods (known as freight) by water was much easier than transporting over land. In local waters, special river and coastal craft were developed to carry freight. Sailing barges hauled coal, flour and other cargoes up and down shallow waterways.

For hundreds of years, a sailor's life was very hard. All kinds of weather had to be endured, from scorching heat to temperatures below freezing. He would have to climb up slippery ropes high above the deck, to haul in and tie heavy canvas sails as winds changed or hurricanes blew. If any sailor lost his footing and fell overboard, he was often left to drown.

In every part of the world, boats developed slightly differently, according to the local needs and water and weather conditions. Today, in the Mediterranean, old forms of sailing boats, Arab dhows and feluccas, are still the best form of transport for local cargoes.

Build a catamaran

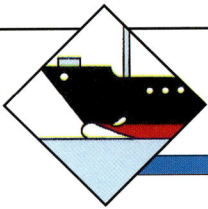

You need:

2 strong plastic detergent bottles
Wood for cross member and stern pieces (400 mm x 75 mm x 15 mm thick)
Dowel (12 mm diameter) about 600 mm long
Wood for mast support (75 mm x 50 mm x 25 mm thick)
Light nylon or plastic material (400 mm x 250 mm)
Stiff wire (2 mm diameter)
1500 mm length thin cord
Large-eye needle
20 drawing pins
2 rubber bands
3 small screw-eyes
Screw-hooks
Junior hacksaw
Hammer
Screwdriver
Modelling knife
Drill
Nails and screws
Sticky tape
Glue
Glass-paper
Modelling clay or Plasticine

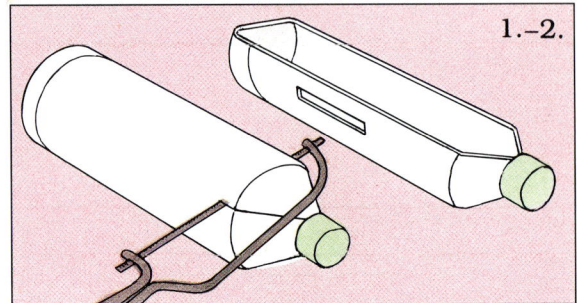

1. Cut down the length of the plastic bottles with the hacksaw. Make sure you leave the caps intact, as shown. Smooth the surfaces with glass-paper.

2. Mark out and cut slots for the wooden cross member, where shown.

3. Use the hacksaw and glass-paper to cut and shape two wooden stern pieces to fit the bottle bases. Knock in drawing pins to make the sail anchoring pins. Use glue to fix the pins.

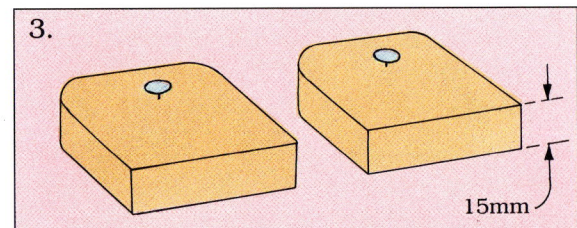

4. Cut and shape the mast support. Drill a 12-mm hole for the mast. Drill another hole behind this for the rudder. Use glue and two screws to fix the mast support to the cross member.

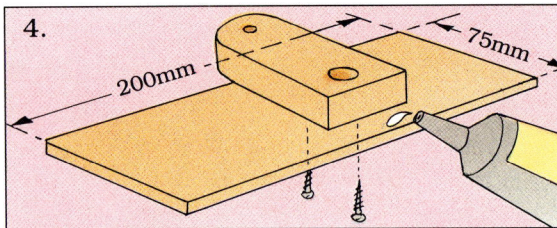

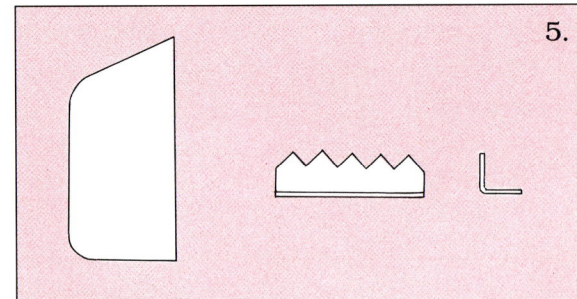

5. Cut out and shape a rudder blade and rudder rack, from left-over plastic-bottle pieces, as shown.

6. Push the 2-mm diameter wire through the hole in the mast support. Bend it into shape for the rudder, as shown. Keep the rudder secure on the mast support by stretching a rubber band across it, held down with two drawing pins. Tape the flat plastic rudder blade in place underneath. Glue the rudder rack in place and secure it with two pins.

7. Glue and pin the boat hulls to the cross member, as shown.

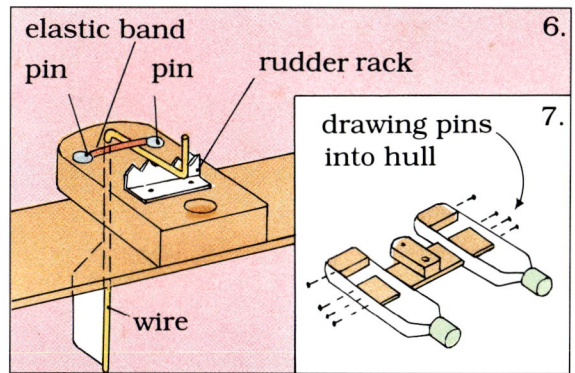

elastic band
pin   pin   rudder rack
6.
drawing pins into hull
7.
wire

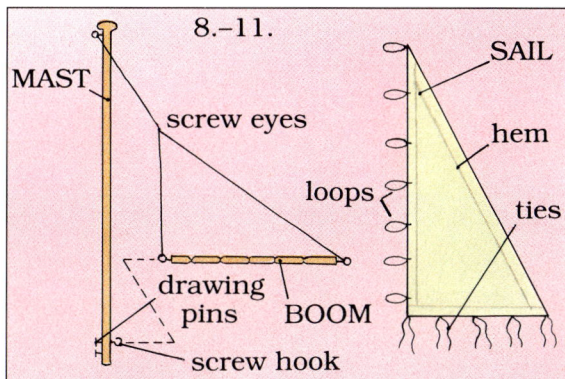

8.–11.

MAST
screw eyes
loops
drawing pins
BOOM
screw hook
SAIL
hem
ties

8. Measure 400 mm along the dowel and cut here to make the mast (400 mm) and boom (200 mm).

9. Cut diagonally across the nylon sheet, to make the triangular sail. Stitch a 15-mm hem all round. Sew thin cord loops on to the mast edge. Sew thin cord ties on to the boom edge of the sail, to secure it on to the boom.

10. Saw tiny notches in the boom, to line up with the sail ties. Drill a tiny hole in each end of the boom and screw an eye into each end.

11. Fix two drawing pins firmly in the lower end of the mast. Drill a tiny hole for a screw eye near the top (for the sail cord). Glue the mast into the mast support and leave to dry.

12. Add clay or Plasticine ballast to each hull until the boat floats evenly. The hulls should be a little more than half submerged.

13. Sail the catamaran on a day with a gentle breeze. Thread the sail on to the mast and boom. Fix the cord on the mast pins. Loop the boom cord to the stern pin. The boom should be set at about 60° angle to the mast. Set the rudder one notch from the centre.

12.–13.

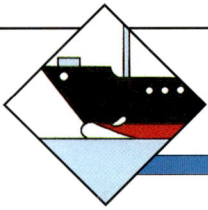

Great sailors

The first ship to circumnavigate (sail around) the world was a sailing ship from the fleet of the Portuguese navigator, Ferdinand Magellan. The fleet set out in 1519, and did not return to Portugal until three years later.

For years before the oceans had been charted, northern sailors searched for the 'north-west passage', that would enable them to sail through to the Pacific Ocean without first going south. To go south meant rounding Cape Horn, the southern tip of South America, which was always an experience that sailors dreaded. Here the perils of the mountainous seas, where two oceans meet, claimed many vessels and their crews.

Between 1882 and 1914 a canal was cut through the narrow land strip of Panama, in Central America. Earlier, in 1869, the Suez Canal between Port Said on the Mediterranean and Suez on the Red Sea, had been completed. These tremendous engineering feats enabled ships to cut their journey times and make safer passages around the world.

Today, the sea still offers the chance of real adventure and new challenges are conquered each year. In 1966 the British sailor, Francis Chichester, successfully sailed around the world single-handedly. Since then a race has been held to see how fast sailors can complete the circumnavigation non-stop.

Yacht-racing is a popular sport with people of all ages and several famous races are held: the Americas Cup, the Fastnet race and the solo Trans-Atlantic races are the best-known. These races make huge physical and mental demands upon the sailors. They have to be able to cope with the roughest of seas in their tiny craft.

The crew of the yacht Maiden *celebrate their win after sailing around the world.*

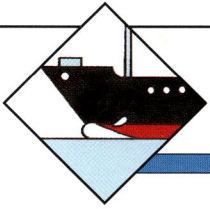

Make a model ship

You need:

A picture of the
   ship you want to
   make, as a guide
Thin strips of balsa wood
Thick cotton thread
Thin card
Thin wire
Rasp or coping saw
Pencil and ruler
Thin dowel for masts
Scissors
Glass-paper
Paints and marker pens

2. Build up the boat hull by gluing together four or five strips of balsa wood. Cut and shape the boat with a coping saw or a rasp. Smooth with glass-paper. Use the card templates to check that the hull is even.

3. Use the thin dowel for the masts and cross-pieces. Drill holes in the deck the right size for the masts. Glue them into the holes. Make other deck fittings, such as cabins, from offcuts of balsa wood.

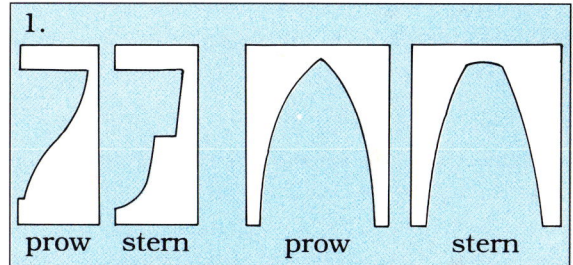

1.

prow   stern   prow   stern

1. Make four templates (patterns) from thin card. Two for the prow and stern profiles. The other two for the prow and stern shapes.

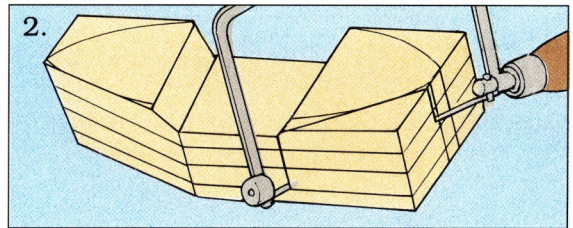

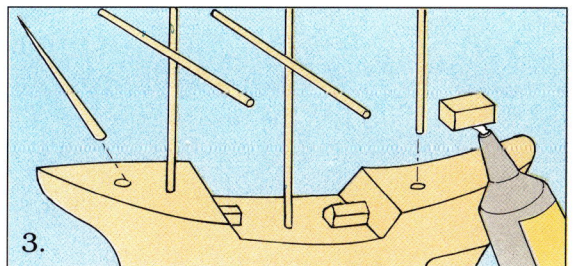

2.

3.

4. Prime and paint the boat. Use a marker pen to draw in timber lines along the sides of the boat and on the deck. Add other details with a marker pen. Cut out sails and a flag from thin card and glue them on to the mast cross-pieces. Make rigging from cotton thread. Attach it to the masts by threading thin wire through and tying it on.

4.

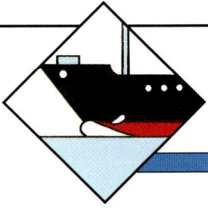

Navigation

Sailors need to know where they are at any time of day or night. Fixing a precise location is known as navigation. Any location can be 'fixed' by two values taken from a standard reference point. Think of the world as a ball, with imaginary lines drawn around it. It has one set of horizontal lines, and one set of vertical lines, evenly spaced. The horizontal lines are called latitude. These start at the Equator as point zero and work up and down towards each pole. The vertical lines are called longitude, starting with zero at Greenwich, England. Each imaginary square has a reference number and navigation is working out which square you are in.

Early sailors navigated by the stars. The pole-star was most favoured in the northern hemisphere and the star pattern known as the Southern Cross was used in the southern hemisphere. The Vikings used lodestones, magnetic

Longitude and Latitude

Lines of latitude

North Pole (90°N)

Equator (0°)

South Pole (90°S)

Lines of longitude

Micro-electronics means small boats can have sophisticated navigation systems.

pieces of rock that constantly pointed in the same direction, as an aid to navigation. The magnetic compass, which continually points to north, is still one of our most valuable navigating instruments.

The lines of longitude divide the world into different time zones. If you travel east, you put your watch forward one hour every time you cross a zone. Travelling west, you lose an hour each time you cross a zone. Establishing the longitude position is done by working out the time difference as you travel away from the zero line at Greenwich. In medieval sailing ships, with only an hour-glass to measure time, accurate positioning was very difficult.

It was not until very accurate time pieces, called chronometers, were built that precision fixing of longitude was achieved.

The sextant is another instrument that is necessary for precise navigation. The sextant establishes longitude, as well as measuring the angles of the sun and the stars against the horizon, to give the latitude position.

In the twentieth century, the advent of radio introduced direction fixes, and ships' positions could be calculated from fixed beacons. Today, the latest technology uses fixed-orbit satellites in space, to give ships constantly monitored positioning.

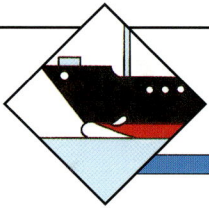

How to take bearings

Sailors draw charts and navigate by taking bearings from fixed landmarks. They use special navigation instruments to do this.

You need:

Simple compass
2 cardboard discs
   (100 mm and
    150 mm in
    diameter)
175-mm length flat
   wood
Dowel (6 mm
   diameter)
    100 mm long

Broom handle,
   150 mm long
2 cotton reels
Junior hacksaw
Glue, sticky tape
Protractor, pencil
   and ruler
Drill

1. Measure and saw 50 mm off the broom handle. Drill a 6-mm hole right through. Push in the dowel so that it fits tightly and sticks out.

2. Glue the flat piece of wood on to the top of this rod. Tape and glue the two cotton reels in position, as shown, so that they line up. These are the sights.

3. Make a small hole in the centre of the small disc. Draw an arrow on it, from the centre to the edge. Push the disc on to the rod, beneath the top assembly gluing it in place with the arrow lining up with the sight tubes.

4. Using the protractor, divide the larger disc into 5° sections. Draw in the sections and number them. Add the directions N.S.W.E. Make a hole in the centre of the disc.

5. Drill a hole 50 mm deep through the remaining length (100 mm) of broom handle. This should be large enough for the dowel to turn in easily. Push the large disc on to the rod. Fix the top assembly (discs, wood and cotton reels) into the broom handle.

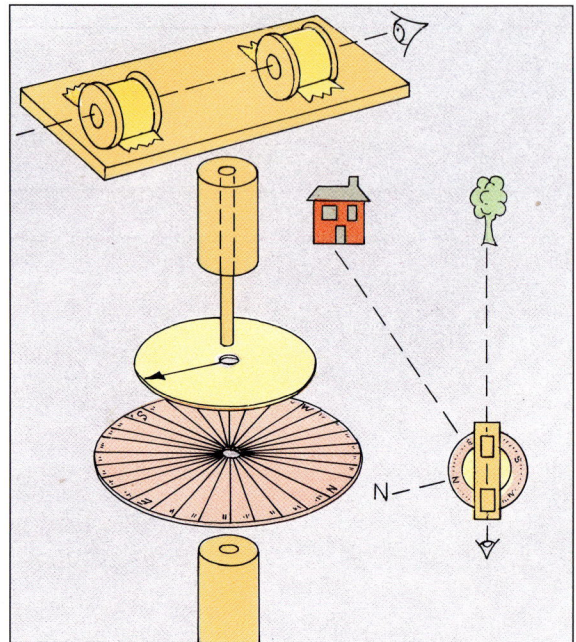

6. Find a good viewing position, with two or three easily identified landmarks close by. Mark your viewing position with stones or a chalk circle, so you can easily find it another day.

7. Hold the broom handle firmly and twist the sight tube to line up with the landmark. Use the compass to find north, and set the large disc to north. Look to see where on the large disc the arrow on the small disc is pointing. Make a note of the reading. Then sight another landmark.

Make a treasure map

You need:

'Parchment' –
  paper aged by
  crumpling it up
  and splashing
  with vinegar
Sighting instru-
  ment
Compass
Drawing pins
'Treasure' – coins
  made from card
  circles
Pencil and paper

1. Choose an area (your garden or the park) and make a sketch map of it. Put in the main landmarks, for example, a pond, flowerbeds, or a clump of trees. Make up names for the landmarks.

2. Decide on a starting point and push a drawing pin into the ground. From the starting point use the compass to find north and mark it on the map. Take a bearing of a landmark. Write down the result and move to a new position.

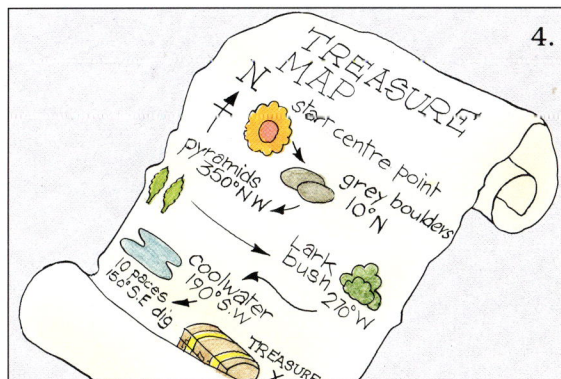

3. Push a drawing pin into the ground at each new position and list the new bearings of landmarks on the map. Do this at least four times to build up a good trail.

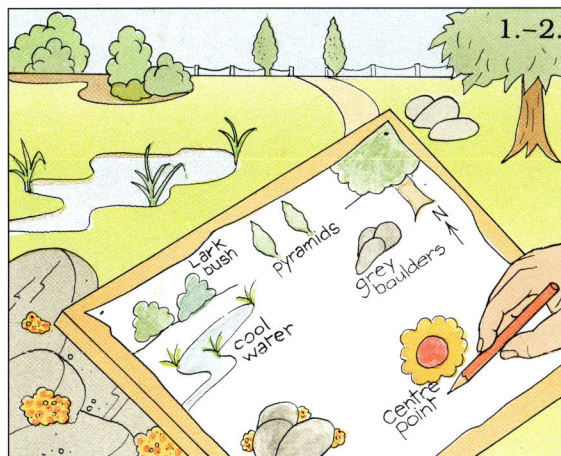

4. Draw up your map on the 'parchment'. Test the map by reading it yourself to make sure it is all correct.

5. Hide the treasure and invite your friends to a treasure hunt.

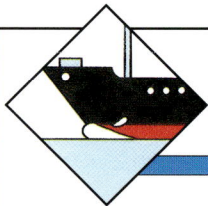

Paddle-steamers

Nineteenth-century Mississippi paddle-steamers travelled far up river.

Early steam-engines were not very reliable. Coal was an expensive alternative to wind power, which was free, and coal took up valuable cargo space. For these reasons it was a long time before nineteenth-century ship owners were persuaded that steamships could be more profitable than sailing-ships.

Initially, vessels that combined both powers were built; steam being used when a boat was in port or when winds were unfavourable. The early steamships had large round wheels with paddles fixed on to either side of the boat. The wheels were driven by a steam-engine located in between. By turning both wheels together, the boat was made to go either forwards or backwards. By turning the paddles in opposite ways, the boat was made to turn very quickly in either direction.

In shallow rivers, paddle-steamers moved freely and American Mississippi stern wheelers are legendary. A hundred years ago, these large flat-bottomed boats hauled huge quantities of freight and passengers up and down the Mississippi river, calling at the busy, crowded ports along the way.

Engineering technology developed very rapidly during the nineteenth century. It was not long before much more efficient and economical engines appeared. Paddles were improved too, those that 'feathered' as they moved through the water made much better use of the available power.

Make a paddle-steamer

You need:

Strong plastic bottle
Dowel (6 mm diameter) 200 mm long
Rubber band
Staple
Screw hooks
Strong thread
Strip balsa wood or correx (wood from fruit boxes)
2 large corks
2 mm diameter stiff wire
Glue
Panel pins
Junior hacksaw
Drill
Small blocks of wood
Clay or Plasticine ballast
Hammer
Glass-paper

1. Saw along the length of the plastic bottle, leaving the cap intact. Glue five wooden blocks for deck supports inside.

2. Drill two holes, one in either side of the hull. Make sure they are large enough for the dowel to turn freely. Hammer the staple into the stern deck support, as shown.

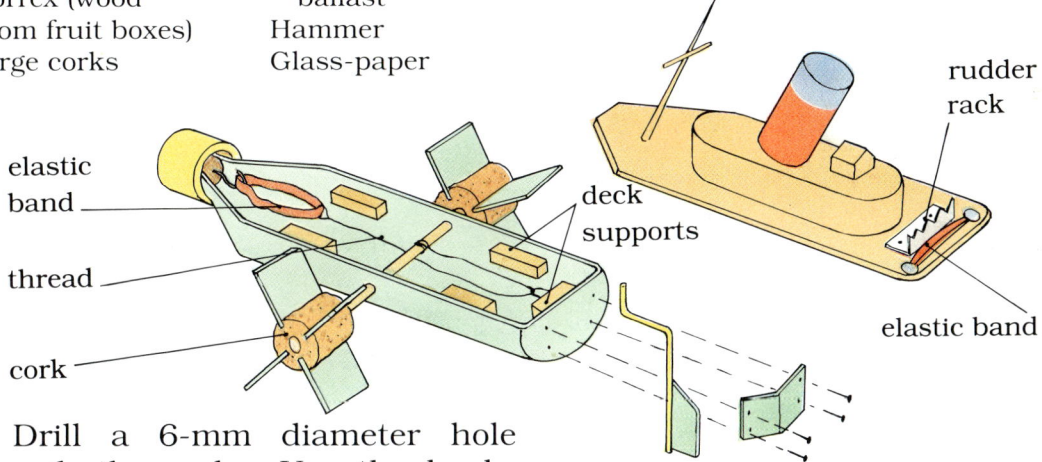

elastic band

thread

cork

deck supports

rudder rack

elastic band

3. Drill a 6-mm diameter hole through the corks. Use the hacksaw to cut four paddle-slots in each cork. Cut out eight paddle blades from the left-over plastic bottle. Slot them into place in the corks. Use glue to ensure they are firmly fixed.

4. Push the dowel through the holes in the boat and fix the cork paddles on to the ends.

5. Knot one end of the thread around the middle of the dowel. Loop the thread through the staple in the stern and tie the other end to the rubber band which is looped over the screw-hook fixed in the cap, as shown.

6. Cut out and shape the deck from balsa wood. Smooth edges with glass-paper. Design and build deck features and glue them on. Fit the deck on to the hull. Do not glue it. Make the rudder and rudder rack (see p.18) and fix it in place.

7. Test the boat by floating it in a bowl of water. Add clay or Plasticine ballast until it floats evenly and half the bottom paddle blade is submerged.

8. Wind the paddles until the rubber band is tight. Put the boat in the water before you let go of the paddles.

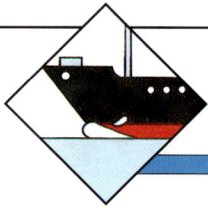

Propellers

The development of the propeller, in about 1850, changed the shape of ships. Rotating a spiral screw shape below the surface of the water meant that almost all the energy from the engines was used to move the boat. By contrast, an old paddle-wheel, at best, had only one-third of its bulk working. Removing the paddles also released a lot more working space in a ship. It was also much easier for the ship to dock, load and unload its cargo.

Three main types of ships were developed: freighters, passenger liners and warships. In the late nineteenth century, refrigeration was introduced into cargo ships, enabling them to transport perishable goods considerable distances. Britain, for example, began to import meat and other goods from New Zealand. At the same time, passenger liners grew larger and more luxurious. However, emergency equipment was poor and it was not until after the sinking of the *Titanic* in 1912, on her maiden voyage, that the minimum number of lifeboats was established.

As passenger liners and cargo ships became larger, they became more difficult to manoeuvre in confined areas. To overcome this problem, small but very powerful tug boats towed ships in and out of port. Often, a harbour pilot operator was also needed to direct large

The nineteenth-century transatlantic liner Campania, *with twin propellers.*

ships between sand banks and along busy shipping lanes. Pilots are still used and today they are taken to and from ships by speedy launches.

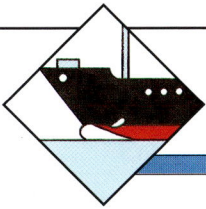

Build a powerboat

You need:

Strong plastic bottle
Propeller shaft and tube (from model shop)
Spring (to fit on shaft and motor spindle)
Electric motor
Battery pack and switch
Balsa wood or correx

22-mm pipe-clip
Small wood blocks
Stiff wire
Clay or Plasticine ballast
Panel pins
Screws
Glue
Drill
Junior hacksaw
Hammer
Glass-paper

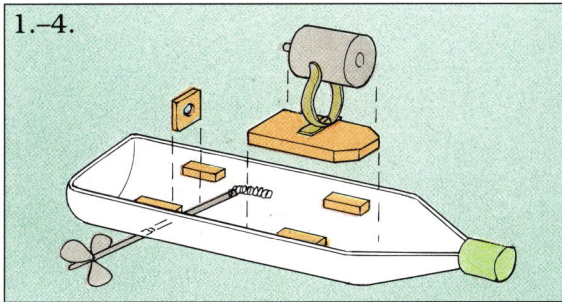

1.–4.

5. Build the rudder as shown, using balsa or correx strips, panel pins, stiff wire and plastic bottle off-cuts. Do not forget the rudder rack. (see p.18)

6. Connect up the motor, as shown in the circuit diagram. (If the boat goes backwards, swap the motor wires around.)

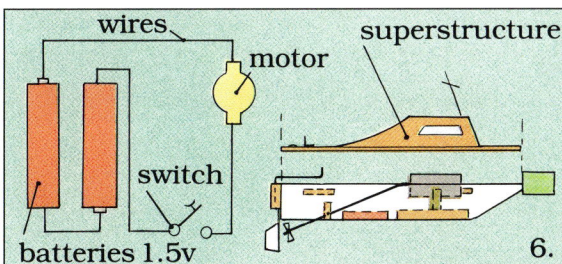

wires, motor, superstructure, switch, batteries 1.5v, 6.

1. Cut down the length of the bottle with a junior hacksaw. Leave the cap intact. Glue the deck supports (four pieces of wood) in position.

2. Cut and shape the engine mounting block from a piece of wood. It should fit the hull and should be large enough to take the pipe clip and motor. Glue it in place. Gluc thc pipc clip in position. Make sure it is central. Cut and shape the stern block from wood and glue in place. Push the motor into the clip.

3. Drill a hole through the hull, to take the propeller tube (as shown in the drawing). Glue the propeller tube in place so that the top is above the water line.

4. Connect the motor to the propeller shaft with the spring.

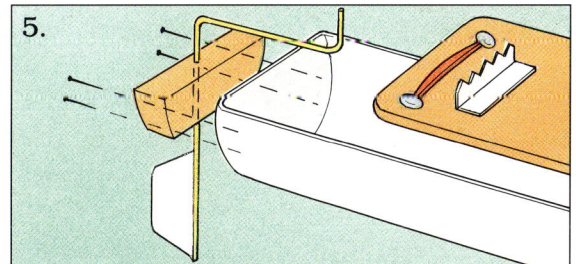

5.

7. Build the superstructure from balsa wood or correx. Fix on the rudder rack. Fit, but do not glue, the superstructure in place.

8. Ballast the boat by slowly adding clay or Plasticine until half the hull lies evenly below water. Set the rudder and start the motor.

Freight carriers

The sea has always provided us with fish to eat, and special fishing vessels have been used to reap their harvest from deep waters. Most commercial fishing nowadays is done by towing large nets behind the boats. The size of the net holes is calculated deliberately to allow the small fish to slip through, escaping until they have grown to full-size.

Where fishing boats are operating a long way from home, they may work in conjunction with a factory ship. The factory ship processes the fish caught by the small boats, at sea. Factory ships may stay at sea for many months, sending home the processed fish and receiving fresh food and equipment from supply ships sent out from the home port.

As the industrialized world has needed more energy, oil has been shipped around the seas. Oil tankers are the largest of our freighters. Carrying many thousands of tonnes of oil in their holds, they must start to slow down out at sea, over a hundred kilometres from the port where they will berth.

Handling goods safely and stowing cargo so that it is not damaged in heavy seas has always been a major problem. Since a ship is likely to change part of its cargo at any port, keeping track of the freight is a skilful task. Packing goods into standard-size containers has revolutionized the docks.

Modern container ships are designed and built specifically to carry these standard container blocks, both below and above decks. Many container ships can sail around the world in less than eighty days.

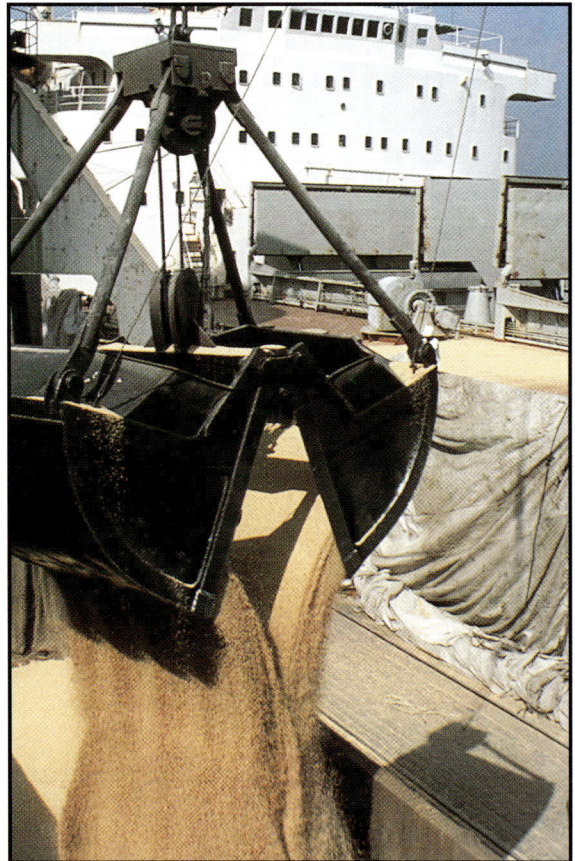

Huge grabs and suction elevators are used to load and unload loose cargoes.

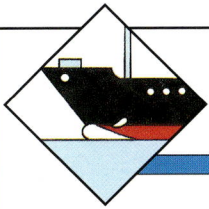

Hydrofoils

The high speed of hydrofoils makes them ideal passenger-ferries.

In comparison to other forms of transport, ships and boats are quite slow. Large ocean liners seldom travel faster than about 56 kph. Freighters are even slower at about 37 kph. Friction between the sides of the boat and the water through which it is passing holds down the speed. The faster a ship travels, the greater the friction becomes and the more energy is used. Scientists worked out that a ship could travel a lot quicker if some of the hull could be lifted out of the water.

Hydrofoils are craft with underwater wings that lift the hull up through the water as they move forwards. The faster they travel, the more lift is exerted and the higher the hull rises out of the water.

There are two types of hydrofoil, the submerged and the vee. Hydrofoil passenger-boats may travel as fast as 96–113 kph, easily making them the fastest general-service boats. Craft with submerged foils need complicated levelling systems to ensure they travel smoothly. In order to maintain a smooth ride, the foil angle is constantly adjusted by electronic signals received from a sonar system that measures the height of the hull above the water. Jet hydrofoils are propelled by water jets. Intakes scoop up the water which is then pumped by powerful gas-turbine engines out of nozzles at the rear end of the boat. In order to maintain a speed of 80 kph, over 100,000 litres of water have to be pumped every minute!

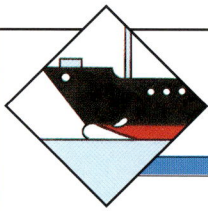

Rescue at sea

Rafts bobbing about in the water are difficult to find. When a rescue plane or ship is spotted by the survivors, smoke flares are released.

Minor boating accidents or major shipping disasters are incidents that threaten human lives. The rescue services must be equipped and on the alert to act immediately in any kind of emergency. Lifeboats and other rescue craft have to be kept in perfect working order and they must be staffed by highly trained and brave crews.

Powerboats, incorporating the latest in speed and boat technology, make very effective rescue craft. They can arrive very quickly on the scene of an accident and take victims speedily back to land.

A major accident at sea might involve calling in the Air Sea Rescue service. Air Sea Rescue works alongside the lifeboat service and has helicopters always at the ready to search for and help distressed craft. It can be difficult to spot people in the sea, so life-jackets and life-rafts are designed to release coloured dye into the water. Victims are winched out of the water and taken aboard the helicopter, where they can be given emergency medical treatment and flown quickly to the nearest hospital.

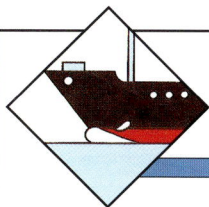

Pleasure boats

Dinghy sailing is an excellent way to learn the sport. A wide variety of classes is available, and even the smallest boats can compete in international events.

Many people today go boating for pleasure. They may choose sailing or power boating, in craft built from traditional or modern materials. The simplest sailing craft are wind surfers and small dinghies. The biggest pleasure boats are cabin craft and large yachts with several masts. Most keen sailors belong to sailing clubs which hold regular competitions.

The best way to learn to sail is to join a club. You can try out different types of craft at a club before going to the expense of buying your own boat. Start first on a small sailing dinghy and learn the important technical terms. As your skill and confidence grow, you will probably have the opportunity to crew on larger vessels. If you crew for experienced skippers who have a good reputation, you will learn good sailing practice. All boats require constant maintenance and they also have to be either moored, parked or trailed home after use.

Always remember that water can be dangerous. Never ever put out in a boat that is not in good order. Prepare to sail in new waters with great care. Find out as much reliable local information as you can from professional sailors. Always wear an approved life-preserver and tell an adult about your planned trip, where you are going, and when you expect to return.

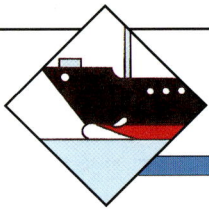

Engines

Built exclusively for racing, power boats flash across the waves.

Boat engines fall mainly into two categories: inboard and outboard.

Inboard engines are fitted within the hull of the boat and connected to the propeller via a shaft through the hull. Inboard engines use either petrol or diesel fuel. Diesel is safer, but the engines are more expensive.

An outboard motor is a complete unit that bolts on to the stern of a boat. Outboard motors are available in many sizes, from small ones for rowing boats or as standby engines for sailing boats, to huge powerful units for driving power-boats. It is also quite common to see pairs of outboards on rescue and racing boats.

Each type of motor has its advantages: inboards can be mounted so that the weight of the engine is down low in the centre of the hull, while outboards can be tilted so that the propellers are lifted clear of the water. A compromise system is called a stern drive, where an inboard engine drives an outboard-style propeller unit. Another popular system is called the jet drive. Here, the inboard engine sucks in water and pushes it out of the rear of the boat as a powerful water jet.

No one should ever venture out in a boat unless the engine is in good working order and properly serviced. It is worth remembering a few safety rules when motor boating. Always check with local professional sources for information about currents or rip-tides, in case the engine on your boat may not be powerful enough to cope with them. Always wear an approved life preserver, and if you are boating out to sea, first ask an adult's permission, pack fresh distress flares and tell the adult when you are due back on shore.

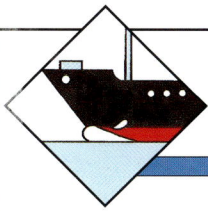

A candle-powered boat

You need:
Piece of wood (250 mm x 100 mm x 25 mm thick)
250 mm copper tubing (3 mm diameter)
1 night-light candle
Paper and pencil
Scissors
Coping saw
Rasp   Drill
Glass-paper
Wood or metal rod (25 mm diameter)

1. Make a template. Fold the sheet of paper in half. Draw half the hull-shape, as shown. Cut out with scissors and unfold.

2. Lay the template on the wood and draw around it. Cut the wood into shape with a coping saw. Smooth and round the edges with a rasp and glass-paper.

3. Measure half-way along the copper tube. Put the rod firmly against the tube at this centre point. Bend the copper tube around the rod 1½ times. Slide the tube off the rod.

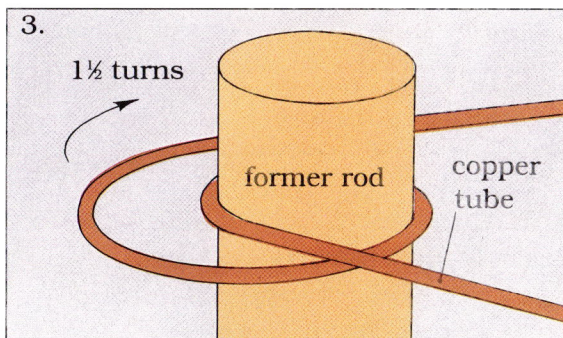

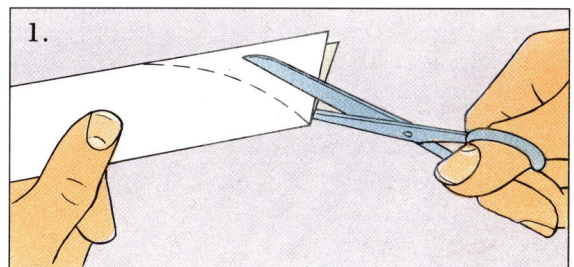

4. At the stern of the boat, mark two holes the right distance apart to take the copper tubing. Drill the holes through from the top at an angle of about 30°, as shown. Do not make the holes too big, the tubing should fit tightly.

5. Push the tubing into the holes until the ends are submerged in water. Saw the ends to equal length and make sure the tubes are not blocked.

6. Glue the candle in place underneath the tube coil. Place the boat in water. Light the candle and wait a few moments. The boat should start to move.

3.
1½ turns
former rod
copper tube

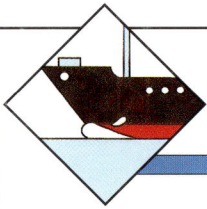

Inland waterways

In the past, transporting heavy loads by water was a very efficient system, but restricted to coastal towns or those alongside large rivers. Although artificial waterways had existed for some time, it was not until the seventeenth century that European countries like Britain and France developed a system of canals specifically for transporting goods. The waterways were great feats of engineering, dug by gangs of workers.

Ingenious systems were employed so canals could cross the countryside. Flights of locks lifted canal boats up and down hills and tunnels were cut through mountains. Huge tanks filled with water, called caissons, operated like lifts to raise and lower boats between different water levels. Perhaps the most spectacular engineering feat of all, was the aqueducts (water-carrying bridges) that crossed valleys.

To begin with, the canal boats were pulled along by horses plodding along a tow path. When a tunnel was encountered, the horse would be unharnessed and walked over the hill. The boat was 'walked' through the tunnel by men lying on the deck and pushing with their feet against the low tunnel roof. At some places, men and boys made a living 'legging' the boat through the tunnel.

When small engines became reliable, canal boats were normally worked in pairs. On board the larger boats there were cramped living quarters for the boatman and his family. Canal boats were often beautifully maintained and gaily painted with traditional decorations of castles and roses.

Canals are still used to transport goods. Here we see a modern cargo ship on Canada's Welland Canal.

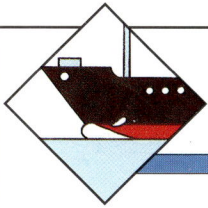

Build a lifting bridge

You need:
2 wooden uprights
(200 mm x
50 mm x 25 mm)
Plywood (150 mm x
100 mm x 6 mm)
2 wooden arms
(300 mm x 25
mm x 12 mm)
2 wooden bridge
walls (150 mm x
25 mm x 12 mm)
Plywood baseboard
(250 mm square
x 6 mm)
Dowel (125 mm x
6 mm diameter)
Plastic box (about
100 mm x 50 mm)
Dry sand
Strong cord
Drill
Hammer
Screws
Nails
Glue

Where roads meet canals there must be bridges. If a bridge is too low for large boats to pass under, then it must either swing or lift out of the way.

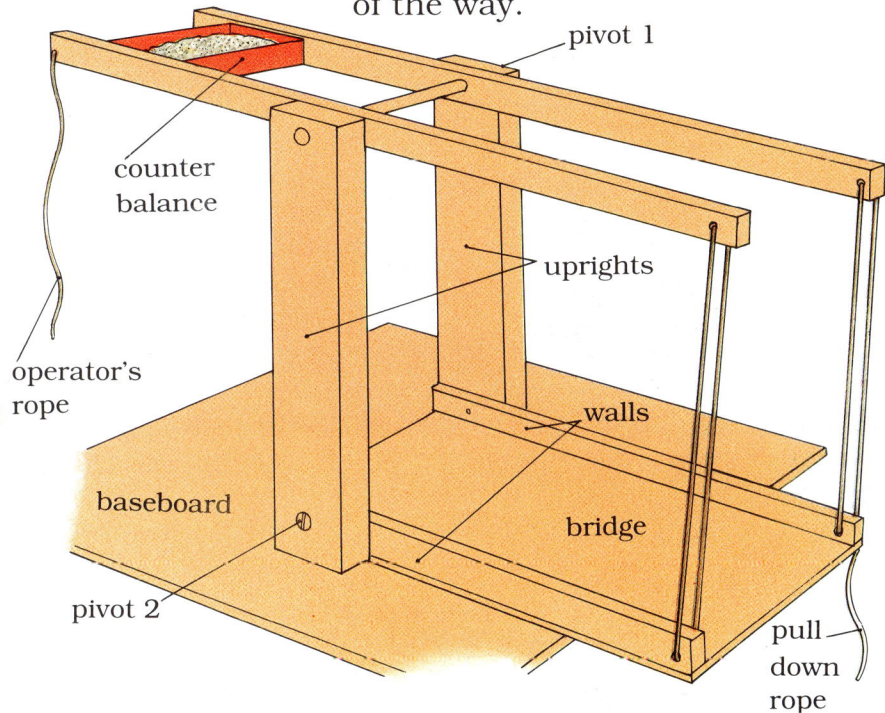

counter balance

operator's rope

pivot 1

uprights

walls

baseboard

bridge

pivot 2

pull down rope

1. Hold uprights firmly together in a vice, if possible. Drill a 6-mm hole through the top of each upright to take the dowel (pivots).
2. Glue or nail the walls to the bridge. Drill a hole in each wall (pivot 2 in drawing). Fit screws through holes into uprights.
3. Screw the baseboard from underneath, to the uprights. Drill 6-mm holes in the arms for the dowel to fit through (pivots). Drill a hole at the other end of each arm

to take the lifting ropes. Push the dowel through the uprights and arms. Drill two more holes. One in the arm that takes the operator's rope, and one in the bridge, for the pull-down ropes.
4. Glue the plastic box between the arms. Set the arms level and thread the lifting ropes through the holes in the ends. Gradually add sand to the plastic box until the bridge will open at only a slight pressure on the rope.

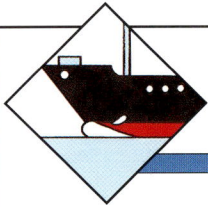

Special boats

Supply ships in the polar regions must cope with frozen seas.

During the winter, ports in northern countries need to keep trading for as long as possible, and sea lanes are kept open by ice-breaker ships. These ships are built with very heavy, rounded bows, to ride up onto the ice until the boat's weight breaks a channel, along which other ships can follow.

In the Florida Everglades, special swamp boats have been developed. Designed to skim over the surface of very shallow water and marshland, these boats are powered by aeroplane-type propellers. Vanes (flat blades) behind the propeller direct the air and steer these fast boats.

In the past, in places where there was no space to build an aircraft runway, sea-planes, or flying boats, were sometimes used. The fuselage of the plane was shaped like a boat hull and any stretch of smooth water was suitable as a runway. The *Catalina* and the *Sunderland* were perhaps the most successful of the flying boats, which were most common in the 1950s. Today, a flying boat is a rare sight, but planes with floats are still used to reach remote communities. These float planes are much cheaper to run than helicopters.

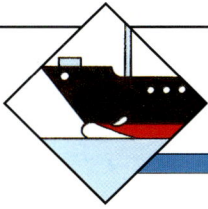

Build a swamp buggy

You need:

Polystyrene food
  tray
Electric motor
Battery pack and
  wires
Switch
Small aero pro-
  peller (from

  model shop)
Thin alloy or stiff
  plastic sheet
Waterproof sticky
  tape
Stiff wire
Pencil and ruler
Scissors

1.–3.

1. Draw and cut out the shape, as shown, for the motor tower from the metal or plastic sheet.

2. Make a hole through the top of the motor tower, for the motor clamp. Fold and bend the motor tower into shape. Screw the motor clamp in position.

3. Push the propeller on to the motor. Fit the motor in the clamp.

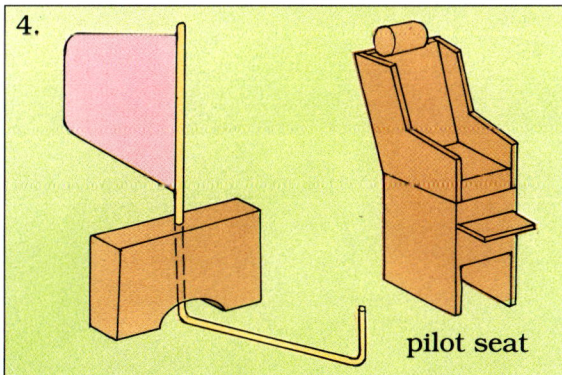

4. Construct a direction vane from stiff wire and plastic offcuts. Glue it in place. Design and build a pilot seat from scrap materials.

5. Wire the motor circuit. (For details, look at the powerboat project p.18).

6. Make and fit a rack (see p.18) for the direction vane.

4.

pilot seat

7. Float the polystyrene tray on water. Balance the motor tower, battery pack and seat on the tray so that the boat floats level. Mark where the different pieces go.

8. Out of the water, tape the tower, battery pack and seat in place. Test the boat on calm water.

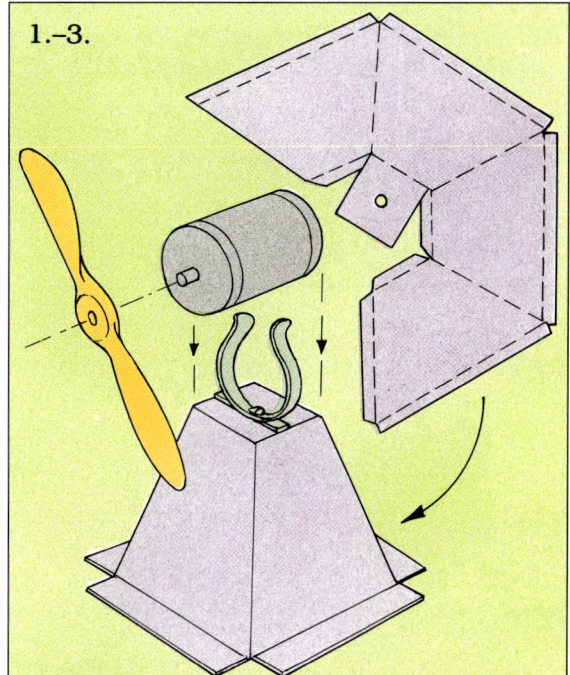

8.

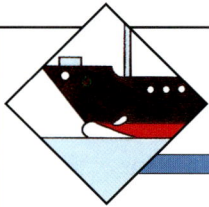

Submarines

Submarines were first used for military purposes by Americans in 1776 when a small submarine called the *Turtle* tried to sink a British warship by screwing explosives to its hull. In 1880, an American, Robert Fuller, built a submarine called *Nautilus*. It had a crew of three and could stay submerged for four hours.

Submarines are unlike other craft. A submarine is really an airtight container inside a watertight container, with tunnels that can be sealed off, leading to the outside. When the tunnel hatchways are closed and water is allowed into the space between the two containers, known as the ballast tanks, the submarine will dive. When air is pumped into the ballast tanks pushing the water out, the submarine will surface. By adjusting the amount of water in the ballast tanks, the depth the submarine floats at can be altered. Underwater, electric motors driven by batteries power the propellers. On the sea surface, diesel engines take over to power the propellers, recharge the batteries and compress the air necessary to empty the ballast tanks.

A device called a periscope enables the submarine to remain submerged and, at the same time, see what is happening on the surface. The periscope is a pipe which is extended up through the water and above the surface. Down in the submarine, the operator can survey the surface by looking into an eyepiece.

Nuclear power has greatly increased the capabilities of submarines. They are now able to travel thousands of kilometres under the sea and stay submerged for several months at a time. Computer-controlled navigation equipment is used to plot faraway underwater locations.

Submarines are also used for exploration work and for the maintenance of oil rigs, pipelines and power cables that lie deep underwater.

A nuclear submarine surfaces.

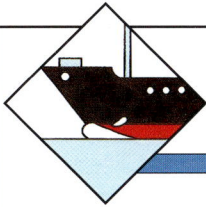

Make a bathyscaphe

You need:

Small plastic bottle
Round plastic film
    case
Balloon
Cork to fit bottle
Empty detergent
    bottle
Length of thin
    plastic tubing
Plastic straws
Blutack
Glue
Sticky tape
Rasp
Modelling knife
Glass-paper

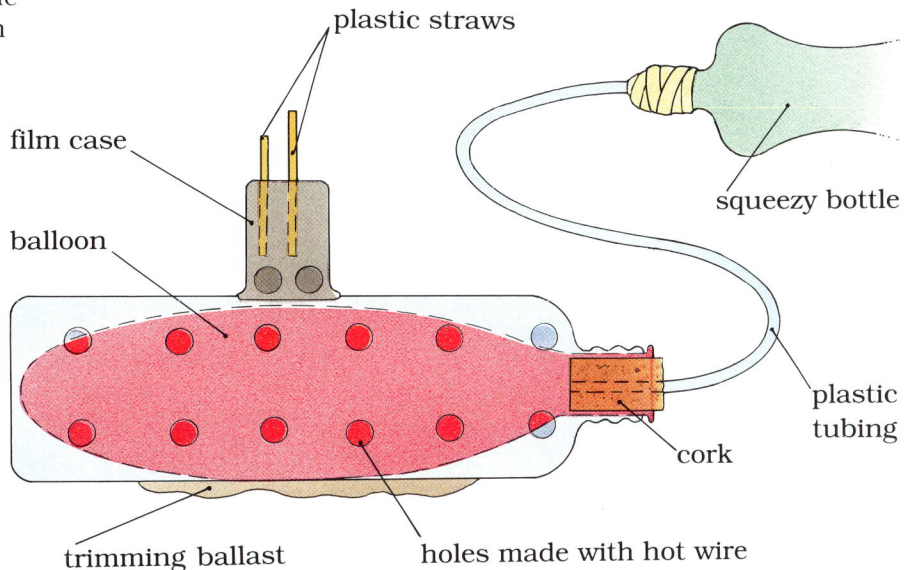

plastic straws

film case

balloon

squeezy bottle

plastic
tubing

cork

trimming ballast

holes made with hot wire

1. Make evenly spaced holes in the plastic bottle. **AN ADULT SHOULD HELP YOU WITH THIS. USE A HEATED NAIL, STUCK IN A CORK, OR HELD WITH PLIERS, OR A SOLDERING IRON.**

2. Use the rasp or modelling knife to cut and shape the film case to fit the bottle. Make holes with the hot nail or soldering iron in the top of the film case for the water drain and periscope pipes (made from plastic straws). Glue the film case to the bottle.

3. Blow up the balloon, then deflate it so that it is stretched. Drill a hole through the cork large enough to push the plastic tubing through. Fit the balloon over the cork and push it inside the bottle.

4. Push the plastic tubing through the cork. Tape the other end of the tubing over the nozzle of the detergent bottle.

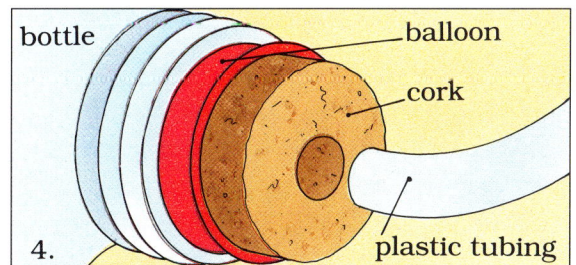

bottle

balloon

cork

4.

plastic tubing

5. Test the bathyscaphe in the bath. Stick Blutack ballast on to the base to make it lie evenly and so that it slowly sinks. Squeeze the detergent bottle. The bathyscaphe will surface as the balloon inflates and submerge as the balloon deflates.

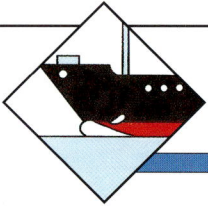

Amphibious craft

Large hovercraft can ferry passengers and cars speedily.

There have been many attempts to develop vehicles that will travel equally well on land and water. Perhaps the most successful example is the hovercraft developed in 1954 by the scientist, Christopher Cockerell. However, the hovercraft lacks the stability on land that wheels give.

Several military vehicles have been built, including the DUKW, which worked with some success but used too much petrol. Tanks and troop carriers have been built with canvas extensions fixed around them, so that they can be floated across canals and rivers, but these are only temporary fittings. In the 1960s, an amphibious car was made that could be driven on land and had propellers to power it through water, but only a few were constructed.

The most common of the current dual-purpose vehicles, are known as ATVs (All Terrain Vehicles). These multi-wheel craft are intended for agricultural work. They can cross firm and soft ground and travel on water. They have balloon-type tyres, which act as floats, and tyre ribs, which work like paddles. Similar special-purpose craft are sometimes used to harvest marshland reeds, or to carry heavy loads over watery or swampy ground.

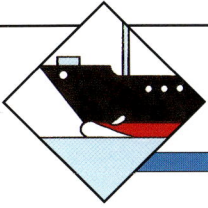

Build a hovercraft

You need

Balloon
15 mm length of dowel, wide enough for the balloon neck to fit tightly over
Small polystyrene food tray or circle of stiff card (125 mm diameter)
Round file
Drill

1. Cut a groove in the dowel, using the round file, as shown.

2. Drill a tiny hole through the centre of the dowel. Start with a 1.5 mm diameter hole and make it larger if you need to.

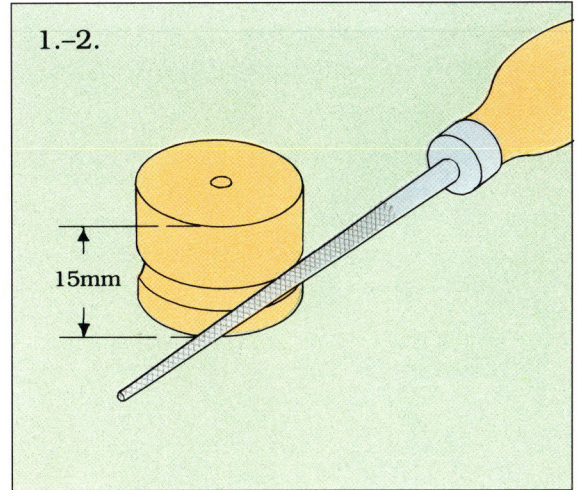

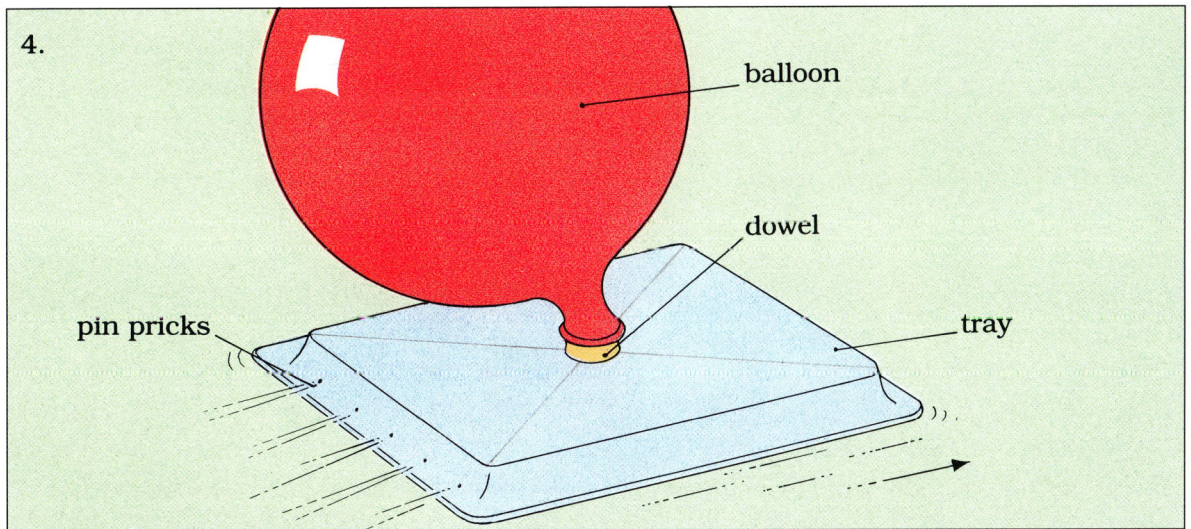

1.–2.

15mm

4.

balloon

dowel

tray

pin pricks

3. Find the exact centre of the tray by drawing diagonal lines from corner to corner – the centre is the point where the lines cross. Glue the dowel to the base of the tray.

4. When dry, drill through the hole in the dowel into the tray. Inflate the balloon and fit the neck over the dowel. The tray should now be hovering over a flat surface. If the tray does not hover, make the hole bigger by 0.5 mm at a time, testing each time.

5. Prick holes in one end of the tray for propulsion jets. Paint the body with water-base paints.

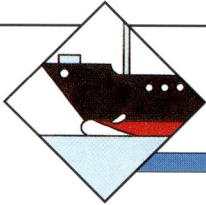

Glossary

Aqueduct Artificial raised channel used to carry water across a valley.

Berth To tie up, or moor a boat or ship in a suitable place.

Bow Front end of a boat or ship.

Buoy An anchored float used as an aid to navigation.

Canal Man-made waterway for inland navigation.

Cargo Goods carried by ship.

Compass Instrument with a needle that always shows magnetic north, and marked with the bearings from it.

Feather To turn an oar or paddle so that it passes through the air edgeways.

Freight Transported goods.

Fuselage Aircraft body.

Harbour Place of shelter for ships.

Hold Space below deck to store ship's cargo.

Hull Body of ship.

Keel Main lengthways structural part of a ship (counterbalanced to the sails).

Landmark Conspicuous feature.

Latitude The distance measured in degrees, north or south of the imaginary line, the Equator.

Lock Section of canal confined within sluice gates, for moving boats from one level to another.

Longitude The distance, measured in degrees, east or west of the imaginary line through Greenwich, England.

Navigation Working out a ship's position, or course.

Oar Pole with blade attached, used to propel a boat through the water by leverage.

Outrigger An additional float to one or both sides of a boat, usually on a canoe.

Paddle A broad blade used to propel a boat through the water.

Pilot The person in charge of a boat entering or leaving a harbour.

Propeller A revolving device with blades, that propels a boat.

Rip-tide A strong current on the sea surface which flows out to sea from the shore.

Sextant An instrument for navigating by the sun and stars.

Skiff A small, lightweight rowing boat with a sliding seat.

Spar A stout wooden pole.

Stern The rear end of a boat or ship.

Superstructure The top part of a ship.

Tacking Changing the course of the boat by turning into the wind in a zig-zag fashion.

Tow path The path beside a canal or river along which horses used to tow barges.

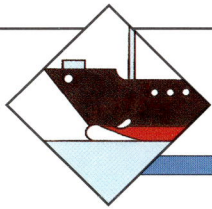

Further Information

Books to read

Barrett, N *Canoeing* (Franklin Watts, 1987)
Cook, J and Way, P *Usborne Book of Windsurfing* (Usborne, 1990)
Dahl, N *Small Boat Sailing* (A & C Black, 1979)
Grey, M *Ships and Submarines* (Franklin Watts, 1986)
Holden, P *Wind and Surf* (Wayland, 1991)
Johnson, H *Land and Sea Transport* (Franklin Watts/Gloucester Press, 1989)
Lambert, M *Ship Technology* (Wayland, 1989)

Action Sports – Windsurfing (Hamish Hamilton, 1986)
Children's Factfinder (Kingfisher, 1985)
Janes Directories of Ships (published annually)
Reverse Dictionary (Readers Digest, 1989)

Organizations to contact

UK
Royal National Lifeboat Institute
West Quay Road
Poole
Dorset BH15 H1Z

Royal Yachting Association
RYA House
Romsey Road
Eastleigh
Hampshire SO5 4YA

The Inland Waterways Association
114 Regents Park Road
London NW1 8UQ

Australia
Port authorities in the capital city of each state.

Canada
Canadian Yachting Association
333 River Road
(11th Floor)
Vanier
Ottawa
Ontario K1L 8B9

Remember to send a stamped, self-addressed envelope with your enquiry.

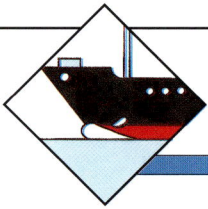

Places to visit

UK
National Waterways Museum
Llanthony Warehouse
Gloucester Docks
Gloucester GL1 2EH

National Maritime Museum
Greenwich
London SE10 9NF

Ironbridge
Museum of the Water
Telford
Shropshire TF8 7AW

Royal National Lifeboat Institution
Museum
Grand Parade
Eastbourne
East Sussex

Mary Rose Ship
Portsmouth Naval Base
HM Naval Base
Portsmouth
Hampshire PO1 3LX

Australia
Port of Echuca
PO Box 35
Echuca
Victoria 3564

Western Australia Maritime
Museum
Cliff Street
Fremantle
Western Australia 6160

Canada
Kanawa International Museum
of Canoes, Kayaks and Rowing
Craft
Toronto
Ontario

Maritime Museum of British
Columbia
Victoria
British Columbia

National Curriculum

This book will be useful to teachers in implementing the National Curriculum at Key Stages 2 and 3. The information and activities relate to:

Technology attainment targets 1, 2, 3 and 4.

Science attainment targets 1, 10, 13.

Water Transport could also be developed as a cross-curricular topic that includes National Curriculum English, Geography, History and Mathematics.

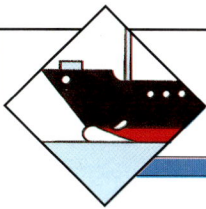

Equipment

All the projects can be made with simple hand tools.

Junior hacksaws are good for cutting both wood and metal. Blades need to be sharp and secure in the frame with the teeth pointing forwards.

Panel-pin hammers are the easiest for small hands to use.

A wheel-brace hand drill and a selection of drill bits (2 mm to 9 mm) will make essential holes. Beware: small drills will cut through steel, but will break if not used with care!

A small file can be used to shape metal or plastic and will smooth wood.

Combination pliers are good for cutting, bending, twisting and holding.

Screws may be either slotted or crosshead, so a screwdriver to suit each sort is essential. Pick ones with comfortable handles that are not too large for the screws you will use.

Some form of work-holding device will make any project very much easier. Gee cramps, a small clamp-on table vice, or a work platform are good choices.

You may have to buy wood. Try to do this economically by setting out shapes on paper first, but remember that it is easier to make straight, rather than jigsaw-type cuts. Check also to see if the grain direction of the timber is important. It might also be more efficient to stock up for two or three projects at once.

Dowel rod is used for axles and pivots. The most common size is 6 mm.

Metal may be more difficult to obtain. Most small engineering firms have a scrap box that will yield suitable lightweight sections, but be very careful of sharp edges.

Join metal pieces with nuts and bolts.

Join timber with screws, panel pins and woodworking glue. PVA glue is excellent, but it must be squeezed tight with pins, screws or cramps and left overnight to dry.

For a smooth finish, use glass-paper on wood and emery cloth on metal.

Apply colour to wood with colouring felts, or acrylic 100 paints that enable brushes to be washed in water. Use an exterior-quality paint for metalwork or models that may be exposed to the weather.

All work should be carried out on a secure, steady surface. Protect the work surface with newspaper. Keep your tools in good order by storing them in a tool storage unit.

Picture acknowledgements

The photographs in this book were supplied by: Allsport 14, 20, 23, 34; Bruce Coleman Ltd 6, 12; Mansell 16; Mary Evans Picture Library 28; PHOTRI 32; Sporting Pictures (UK) Ltd *front cover;* Topham 8, 17, 30, 38, 40; Wayland Picture Library 4, 26, 31, 37, 42; ZEFA 33. All illustrations by John Yates.

Index